Cycles, Cycles, C...

Written and Illustrated

By

Michael Elsohn Ross

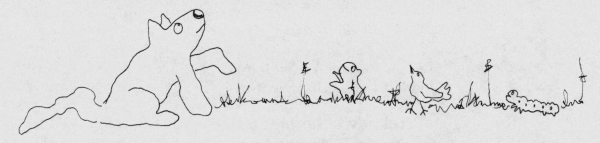

Published by

Yosemite Natural History Association

© 1979

Dedicated to
my nieces
Kolina Jane and Mimi Kara
and the cycles in your lives

Acknowledgements

Many thanks to Henry Berrey, Blue
and Phil Tierney, Arnold Schultz,
Maurice Sendak and my family for
their suggestions and encouragement.
Special thanks to Lisa Rhudy and
Phyllis Weber for all the wonderful
advice.

Contents

What are cycles . . .   4

Apple life cycle   9

Bug life cycle 24

Water cycle 39

Calcium cycle 59

Decomposition cycle 70

The earth 78

Book cycle 83

This is going to be a book about cycles.   **What are cycles?**

4

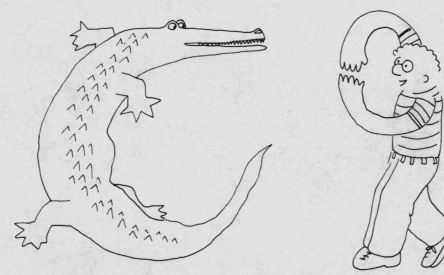

I think they are something that go around and around.

Cycles make circles.

5

Is my bicycle a kind of cycle?   **A bicycle has two wheels that go around.**   **It has two cycles.**

6

Are there other cycles besides motorcycles, tricycles, and unicycles?

Yes, there are many.

If you read this book you
can learn about many cycles.

I'll read it if you help me.

Apple life cycle

Have you ever heard of life cycles?

No. What is a life cycle?

A life cycle is life going in circles.

11

We can begin finding out about life cycles by using an apple.

Inside an apple are seeds.

If you plant a seed in a sunny place and water it...

It will grow...

15

And grow!

16

When you are in high school

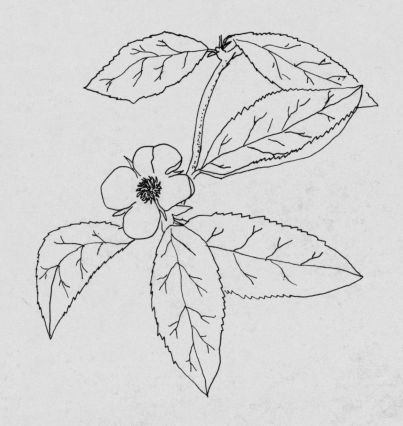

the tree will begin to flower.

After the bees visit

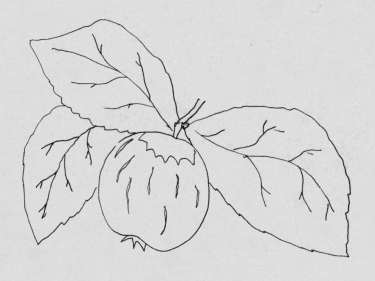

the apple starts to form.

When you finish eating the apple

you can grow another tree.

That is a circle.   **Yes! It is a life cycle, too!**

Bug life cycle

My life cycle goes much faster than the life cycle of an apple.

How long does it take?

25

The life cycle for most of us insects lasts about a month.

There could be 12 cycles a year.

**Our life is so short that
we have to keep busy.**

Busy doing what?

Busy eating leaves   **You are growing!**

And more leaves.   **You are growing more.**

These leaves taste good.   **My! You are getting big.**

I'm so full I think I will
curl up inside a coccoon.

How do you do that?

Like this. **I wonder how long he will be a pupa?**

32

A week passes by and then out of the coccoon pops a...

. . .butterfly!   My! You are pretty.

What are you doing now?   I am drinking nectar so I can fly and find...

. . .my mate and together we will make eggs.

From the eggs will hatch little caterpillars.

Now the life cycle starts all over again. **And I'm sure hungry!**

Water cycle

Have you ever heard of the water cycle?   **No. Who are you?**

I am a drop of water and I have been to a lot of places.

I have been drunk by dinosaurs.

And I have washed floors.

I have been in all the seas.

And I have watered many trees.

And I have been flushed.

Where I have not been I am going to go.

How do you get around?   **It all begins when I get hot.**

What makes you hot?   **Usually the sun.**

49

When I get too hot I turn into vapor and float up and up...

and up until I become part of a cloud.

I will stay in a cloud as long as I am warm.

If I get cold I will fall as a snowflake or raindrop.

53

When I hit the ground I usually run to a stream.

The stream might take me to a river.

If the river goes by a town I might become drinking water.

And then come out your spout.

Here I am again.   **You made a circle.**   **Another cycle.**

Calcium cycle

Do you know that minerals go in cycles too?   **What is a mineral?**

60

Anything that is not a plant or animal, like a rock.

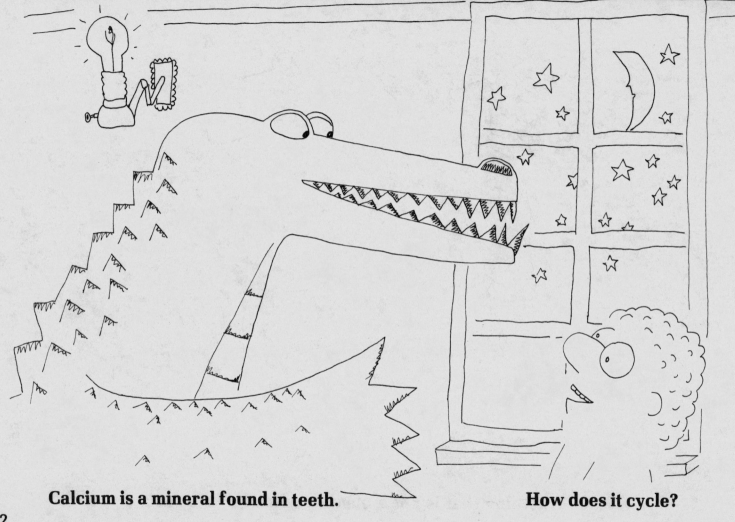

Calcium is a mineral found in teeth.

How does it cycle?

When a tooth falls out
where do you put it?   **Under my pillow.**

63

At night the tooth fairies take the tooth and put it in the ground.

The calcium in the tooth goes in
the grass and helps it grow.

Does it stay there?

65

The calcium stays in the grass until a cow eats the grass.

The calcium will go into the cow's bones and teeth and milk.

If you drink the milk the calcium will go into your body and bones and...

maybe a new tooth.

That is another cycle!

69

"I bequeath myself to the dirt
To grow for the grass I love
If you want to see me again
Look for me under your bootsole."
Walt Whitman

Decomposition cycle

Have you ever heard of the decomposition cycle?   **No. Please tell me about it.**

**Plants and animals are made of elements
such as calcium, carbon, oxygen, and many others.**

Soon after a plant or animal dies it begins to decompose.

Decomposers are plants and animals that help turn dead things into soil.

Plants use elements in the soil to help them grow.

Animals eat the plants and get the elements.

When they die the cycle begins again.

The earth

Did you know that the earth is finite?   **No. What is finite?**

Finite means only a limited size.
The earth is bigger than an elephant and smaller than the sun.

Since the earth is finite it has a limited amount of elements.

Without cycles we would have run out of elements a long time ago.

Book cycle

Is this the end?   **This is the end of the book but not the end of the book's cycle.**

CYCLES HAVE NO BEGINNING AND NO END • CYCLES HAVE NO BEGINNING AND NO END • CYCLES HAVE NO BEGINNING AND NO END • CYCLES HAVE NO BEGINNING AND NO END •

When this book gets old and tattered it will be eaten by bugs

and turned into soil to grow a tree

that might be made into paper for a new book.